Treasury
of
Prayer

Illustrated by Juliette Clarke

First published in Great Britain in 1992 by

PALM TREE
Rattlesden
Bury St Edmunds
Suffolk   IP30 0SZ
England

LUTHERAN PUBLISHING HOUSE
205 Halifax Street
Adelaide
SA 5000
Australia

ISBN 0 86209 325 2

Printed in Hong Kong

Contents

An Introduction to Prayer 5
   The Lord's Prayer 6
   Take time 7
   The Difference 8

Prayers of Love and Peace 9
   Every work of love 9

Love as God's gift
   From a friend 10
   I asked Jesus 12
   Love 12
   The fruit of the Spirit 12

Love as our response
   Friendship 13
   Simple acts of love 13
   Never too busy to care 14
   Someone who cares 14
   Make me willing 14
   A messenger of your love 15
   Prayer of dedication 15

Peace
   Peace 16
   Prayer of Francis of Assisi 16
   Be at peace 16

Patience and Serenity
   Christ is the bridge 17
   Give me patience 18
   God grant me serenity 18
   A prayer for patience 18

Prayers of Trust and Hope 19
   Trust the past 19

As acceptance
   God has not promised 20
   Be still 20

Be at peace 20
The Lord our protector 21
May your love 21
Remind me, Lord 21
Your will for my life 22
Never alone 22
Where God is 22
Help me to accept 23
This is the confidence 23
Safe in God's keeping 23

As active
Lord, your way is perfect 24
Thy will 24
Together 24
Don't quit 25
Everything is possible 25
Trust in God 25
An everyday prayer 26
Jesus is pleased to come 26
Life's lessons 26
A prayer when distracted 27
The Gate of the Year 28
Christ be with me 28
Your will be done 29
I am with you always 29
Wings of Faith 30
The Twenty-Third Psalm 31

In the evening
Safe through the night 32
At the ending of this day 32

Prayers of Joy and Thanksgiving 33
   The day returns 34
   Prayer of Richard of Chichester 34
   God makes the difference 35
   A grateful heart 35
   Love and joy 36

PRAYERS OF SORROW AND ANXIETY	37
The Lord will turn	37
I am with you	38
When dreams are broken	38
Do not be afraid	38
Take courage!	39
You are no stranger	39
Beyond the shadows	39
You are there	40
God is the answer	40
The Divine Weaver	41
Everlasting love	41
Footprints	42

Bereavement

Do not be sad	43
Death is nothing at all	44
Beside the still waters	45
From the Lord of love	46
In comfort and in hope	47
Hold my hand	47
Those who live in the Lord	48
Sympathy	48
Life eternal	48

PRAYERS FOR INDIVIDUALS	
AND FAMILIES	49
Marriage prayer	50
Learning to live	50
Recipe for a happy home	51
Bless our home	51
Kitchen prayer	51
Guide for a loving home	52
If I could	53
A prayer for those who live alone	54
Together we can do	54

BLESSINGS	55
When you're lonely	56
A blessing	56
The peace of God	57
Paul's Farewell	57
Loving care	58
I said a prayer	58
The Beatitudes	59
Deep peace	60
His love	60

An Introduction to Prayer

THE LORD'S PRAYER

Our Father, who art in heaven,
hallowed be thy name.
Thy Kingdom come, thy will be done,
on earth as it is in heaven.

Give us this day our daily bread;
and forgive us our trespasses,
as we forgive those who
trespass against us.

And lead us not into temptation,
but deliver us from evil.
For thine is the Kingdom,
the Power and the Glory,
for ever and ever.

Take Time

Take time to THINK . . .
it is the source of power.
Take time to PLAY . . .
it is the secret of perpetual youth.
Take time to READ . . .
it is the fountain of wisdom.
Take time to PRAY . . .
it is the greatest power on earth.
Take time to LOVE and BE LOVED. . .
it is a God-given privilege.

Take time to BE FRIENDLY . . .
it is the road to happiness.
Take time to LAUGH . . .
it is the music of the soul.
Take time to GIVE . . .
it is too short a day to be selfish.
Take time to WORK . . .
it is the price of success.
Take time to DO CHARITY . . .
it is the key to heaven.

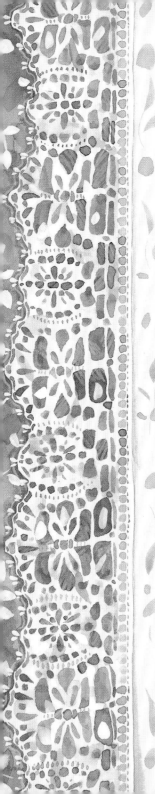

THE DIFFERENCE

I got up early one morning and
rushed right into the day;
I had so much to accomplish that
I didn't have time to pray.
Problems just tumbled about me,
and heavier came each task.
'Why doesn't God help me?' I wondered,
he answered, 'You didn't ask.'

I wanted to see joy and beauty,
but the day toiled on grey and bleak,
I wondered why God didn't show me;
he said, 'You didn't seek.'
I tried to come into God's presence;
I used all my keys at the lock.
God gently and lovingly chided,
'My child, you didn't knock'.

I woke up early this morning,
and paused before entering the day;
I had so much to accomplish
that I had to take time to pray.

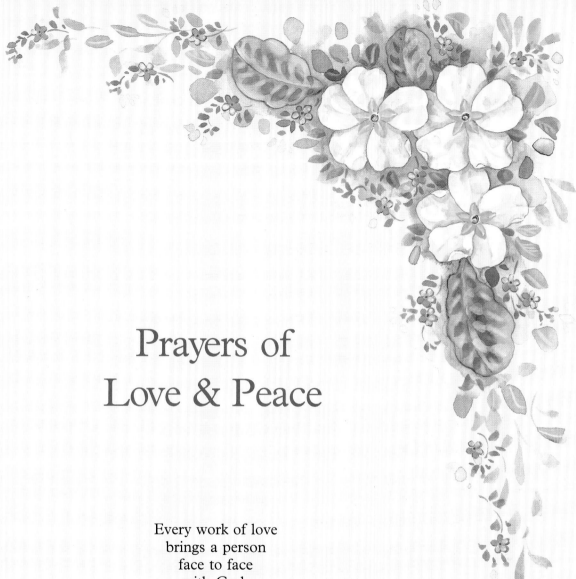

Prayers of
Love & Peace

Every work of love
brings a person
face to face
with God.

MOTHER TERESA

LOVE AS GOD'S GIFT

FROM A FRIEND

Dear Friend,
How are you?
I just had to send a note to tell you
how much I care about you.
I saw you yesterday as you were
talking with your friends;
I waited all day hoping you would
want to talk with me too.
I gave you a sunset to close your day
and a cool breeze to rest you,
and I waited.
You never came.

It hurt me – but I still love you
because I am your friend.
I saw you sleeping last night
and longed to touch your brow,
so I spilled moonlight upon your face.
Again I waited,
wanting to rush down so we could talk.
I have so many gifts for you!
You awoke and rushed off to work.
My tears were in the rain.

If you would only listen to me!
I love you!
I try to tell you in blue skies
and in the quiet green grass.
I whisper it in leaves on the trees
and breathe it in colours of flowers,
shout it to you in mountain streams,
give the birds love songs to sing;
I clothe you with warm sunshine
and perfume the air
with nature's scents.
My love for you is deeper than the ocean
and bigger than the biggest
need in your heart!
Ask me! Talk with me!
Please don't forget me,
I have so much to share with you!
I won't trouble you any further.
It is YOUR decision,
I have chosen you
and I still wait
because I love you.
Your friend,

JESUS.

I Asked Jesus

I asked
JESUS
'How much do
you love me?'
'This much,'
he answered, and
he stretched out
his arms and died.

Love

Love is patient and kind;
it is not jealous or conceited or proud;
Love is not ill-mannered
or selfish or irritable;
Love does not keep a record of wrongs;
Love is not happy with evil
but is happy with the truth.
Love never gives up;
and its faith, hope and patience
never fail.

I Corinthians 13:4-7

The fruit of the Spirit is love,
joy, peace, gentleness, goodness,
faith, meekness, temperance.

Galatians 5:22-23

LOVE AS OUR RESPONSE

FRIENDSHIP

A friend is like a tower strong;
a friend is like the joyous song
that helps us on our way.
When golden ties of friendship bind
the heart to heart, the mind to mind
how fortunate are we!

For friendship is a noble thing;
it soars past death on angel's wing
into eternity.
God blesses friendship's holy bond
both here and in the great beyond:
a benefit unpriced.

Then may we know that wondrous joy,
that precious ore without alloy;
a friendship based on Christ.

Simple acts of love and care
keep the light of Christ burning.

MOTHER TERESA

NEVER TOO BUSY TO CARE

Lord, make me so sensitive
to the needs of those around me
that I never fail to know
when they're hurting or afraid;
or when they're simply crying out
for someone's touch to ease their loneliness.
Let me love so much that my
first thought is of others
and my last thought is of me.

SOMEONE WHO CARES

Lord, make my heart a haven
where the lonely may find friendship,
where the weary may find shelter,
where the helpless may find refuge,
where the hopeless may find hope,
where all those who seek someone who cares
may enter and find you.

MAKE ME WILLING

When I want to do
only great things, Lord,
make me willing to do
small, unnoticed things too.
When I want to do
what the world will acclaim,
make me willing to do
what will lift up your name.

A Messenger of Your Love

Lord, make me a messenger
of your love:
to the searching heart
send me with your word;
to the aching heart
send me with your peace;
to the broken heart
send me with your love.
However small or wide
my world, Lord,
let me warm it with
the promise that you care.

Prayer of Dedication

Lord, Jesus,
I give you my hands to do your work.
I give you my feet to go your way.
I give you my eyes to see as you do.
I give you my tongue
to speak your words.
I give you my mind
that you may think in me.
I give you my spirit
that you may pray in me.

Above all
I give you my heart
that you may love in me,
your Father, and all mankind.
I give you my whole self
that you may grow in me,
so that it is you, Lord Jesus,
who live and work and pray in me.

15

PEACE

PEACE

Lead me from death to life,
from falsehood to truth;
lead me from despair to hope,
from fear to trust.

Lead me from hate to love,
from war to peace;
let your peace fill our hearts,
our lives and our world.

PRAYER OF
FRANCIS OF ASSISI

Lord, make me an
instrument of your peace:
where there is hatred,
let me sow love:
where there is injury, pardon:
where there is doubt, faith:
where there is darkness, light:
where there is despair, hope,
and where there is sadness, joy.

Divine Master, grant that I
may not so much seek to
be consoled as to console,
to be understood as to understand,
to be loved as to love.
For it is in giving that we receive,
it is in pardoning that we
are pardoned,
and in dying that we are
born to eternal life.

Be at peace with one another.

MARK 9:50

PATIENCE AND SERENITY

CHRIST IS THE BRIDGE

Christ is the bridge
that reaches past today and destiny,
to join the things of heaven
with those of earth.
He links
creation's dawning
with infinity's vast shore.

The arch across all history
is his birth.
His cross of love is raised
above a world where war and sin
have torn God
and his children far apart.
It spans the centuries
to give safe passage to his peace.
Christ is the bridge,
the way to God's own heart.

GOD GRANT ME SERENITY

God grant me serenity
to accept the things I cannot change,
courage to change the things I can
and wisdom to know the difference.

A PRAYER FOR PATIENCE

When my patience
seems too short
help me stretch it;
teach me how to meet
a crisis with a smile.
When I'm running out
of quick and clever answers
let the questions stop
for just a little while.

When it seems as though
the day has too few hours
in which to do the things
I have to do,
may I always find the time
for what's important –
time for listening,
time for love
and laughter too.

GIVE ME PATIENCE

It isn't in the quiet,
in the solitude of the study,
that I grow, Lord,
rather at the supermarket checkout
or behind a hopeless traffic jam.
Give me the deep breath of calm
when the clock is racing.

Prayers of Trust & Hope

Trust the past
to the mercy of God,
the present to his love,
the future to his providence.

TRUST AND
HOPE AS ACCEPTANCE

GOD HAS NOT PROMISED

God has not promised
sun without rain,
joy without sorrow,
peace without pain.
But God has promised
strength for the day,
rest for the labour,
light for the way,
grace for the trials,
help from above,
unfailing sympathy,
undying love.

Be still, and know
that I am God.

PSALM 46:10

BE AT PEACE

Do not look forward
to what might happen tomorrow;
the same everlasting Father
who cares for you today
will take care of you
tomorrow and every day.
Be at peace, then, and put aside
all anxious thoughts and imaginings.

FRANCIS DE SALES

THE LORD
OUR PROTECTOR

I lift up my eyes to the hills.
From whence does my help come?
My help comes from the Lord,
who made heaven and earth.

He will not let your foot be moved,
he who keeps you will not slumber.
Behold, he who keeps Israel
will neither slumber nor sleep.

The Lord is your keeper;
the Lord is your shade on your right hand.
The sun shall not smite you by day,
nor the moon by night.

The Lord will keep you from all evil;
he will keep your life.
The Lord will keep your going out and
your coming in,
from this time forth
and for evermore.

PSALM 121

May your love enfold me,
may your peace surround me,
may your light touch me.

REMIND ME, LORD

Remind me, Lord, that your love
is bigger than any problem.
The more I look at the problem,
the bigger the problem becomes.
But when I look to you, Lord,
my anxiety pales
in the light of your love.

Your Will for My Life

You know the deepest wishes
of my heart, Lord,
the cherished dreams,
the silent things
for which we have no voice,
but better still is your will
for my life, Lord.
Let all that comes to me today
be those gifts of your choice.

Never Alone

O Lord,
never let us think that
we can stand
by ourselves
and not need you.

Where God Is

Where there is faith there is love,
where there is love there is peace,
and where there is peace there is God.

HELP ME TO ACCEPT

Help me to accept, Lord,
though I may not understand,
that the landscape of my life
has been designed by your own hand.
It would be a barren place
if storm clouds never came
to enrich and ripen all that grows
with life renewing rain.

This is the confidence
which we have in him
that if we ask anything
according to his will
he hears us.

I JOHN 5:14

SAFE IN GOD'S KEEPING

Look at the sparrows
so small and light,
not one is forgotten
in God's sight.

So rejoice in his love
and take delight.
You are worth more
than hundreds of sparrows.

MATTHEW 10:31

TRUST AND HOPE AS ACTIVE

LORD, YOUR WAY IS PERFECT

Lord, your way is perfect:
help us always to trust in your goodness, so that,
walking with you and following you in all simplicity,
we may possess quiet and contented minds,
and may cast all our care on you,
for you care for us.
Grant this, Lord, for your dear Son's sake,
Jesus Christ.

THY WILL

Help me, when I say, 'Thy will,
not mine,' to really mean it.
Let me remember, Lord,
that my view is narrow,
but yours is all encompassing.
My will is human,
but yours is perfect wisdom.
My thoughts are now,
but your plans eternity.

TOGETHER

Lord, help me remember
that nothing is going to happen today
that you and I cannot handle together.

DON'T QUIT

When things go wrong
as they sometimes will;
when the road you are trudging
seems all uphill;
when funds are low and debts are high
and you want to smile
but you have to sigh;
when care is pressing you down a bit,
rest, if you must,
but don't you quit.

Life is strange
with its twists and turns,
as every one of us sometimes learns,
and many a failure turns about
when they might have won,
had they stuck it out.

Don't give up
though the pace seems slow.
You may succeed with another blow.
Success is failure turned inside out
the silver tint of the cloud of doubt,
and you never can tell
how close you are;
it may be near when it seems so far.

So stick to the fight
when you're hardest hit.
It's when things seem worst
you must not quit.

EVERYTHING IS POSSIBLE

This is impossible
for a human being,
but for God
everything is possible.

MATTHEW 19:26

TRUST IN GOD

Commit your work to the Lord
and then it will succeed.

PROVERBS 16:3

An Everyday Prayer

Lord, in all I do today,
remind me that there's just one way
to do the things that I do best,
to put my mind and heart at rest.
And that's to put in your great hands
my life, that you alone have planned.

Jesus is pleased to come to us
as the truth to be told
and the life to be lived,
as the light to be lighted
and the love to be loved,
as the joy to be given
and the peace to be spread.

MOTHER TERESA

Life's Lessons

After a while
you learn the difference
between holding a hand
and chaining a soul.
You learn that love isn't leaning,
but lending support.
You begin to accept your defeats
with the grace of an adult,
not the grief of a child.

You decide to build
your roads on today,
for tomorrow's ground
is too uncertain.
You help someone plant a garden
instead of waiting
for someone to bring you flowers.
You learn that God has given you
the strength to endure,
and that you really do have worth.

A Prayer When Distracted

When the heart is hard and parched up
come upon me with a shower of mercy.
When grace is lost from life
come with a burst of song.
When tumultuous work
raises its din on all sides,
shutting me out from beyond,
come to me, my Lord of silence,
with thy peace and rest.
When my beggarly heart sits crouched,
shut up in a corner,
break open the door
and come with the ceremony of a king.
When desire blinds the mind
with delusion and dust,
O thou holy one, thou wakeful,
come with thy light and thy thunder.

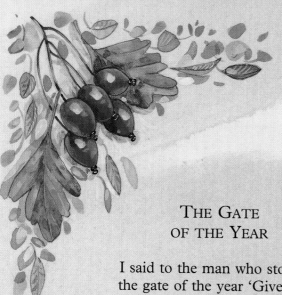

THE GATE
OF THE YEAR

I said to the man who stood at
the gate of the year 'Give me a
light that I may tread safely
into the unknown.'
And he replied – 'Go out into the
darkness and put your hand
into the hand of God.
That shall be to you better than light
and safer than a known way!'

So I went forth and finding the
hand of God, trod gladly into
the night. And he led me
towards the hills and the
breaking of day in the lone East.

MINNIE LOUISE HASKINS

CHRIST
BE WITH ME

Christ be with me,
Christ within me,
Christ behind me,
Christ before me,
Christ beside me,
Christ to win me,
Christ to comfort
and restore me,

Christ beneath me,
Christ above me,
Christ in quiet,
Christ in danger,
Christ in hearts
of all that love me,
Christ in mouth
of friend and stranger.

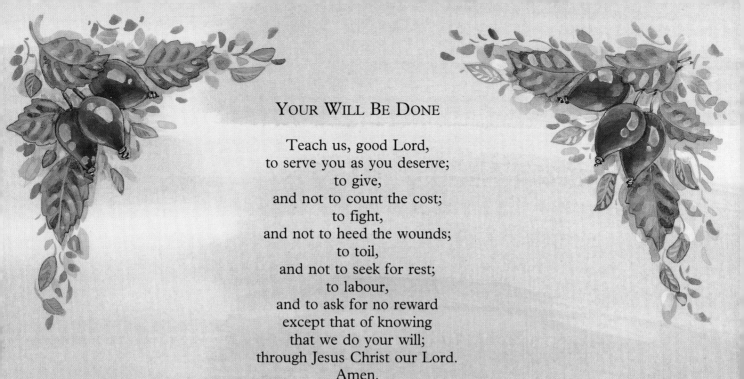

Your Will Be Done

Teach us, good Lord,
to serve you as you deserve;
to give,
and not to count the cost;
to fight,
and not to heed the wounds;
to toil,
and not to seek for rest;
to labour,
and to ask for no reward
except that of knowing
that we do your will;
through Jesus Christ our Lord.
Amen.

I Am With You Always

In the springtime of your life, when joy is new,
and when the summer brings the fullness
of your faith, I'm there with you.
I am with you in the autumn
of your years to turn to gold
every memory of your yesterdays,
to banish winter's cold.
I am with you in the sunshine,
when your world glows warm and bright.
I am with you when life's shadows
bring long hours of endless night.
I am with you every moment,
every hour of every day.
Go in peace upon life's journey,
for I'm with you all the way.

WINGS OF FAITH

Give us, Lord, a special faith,
unlimited and free,
a faith that isn't bound
by what we know or what we see.

A faith that trusts the sunshine
even when there is no light,
a faith that hears the morning song's
soft echo in the night.

A faith that somehow rises
past unhappiness or pain,
knowing that in every loss
your goodness will remain.

A faith that finds your steadfast love
sufficient for all things,
a faith that lifts the heart above
and gives the spirit wings.

THE
TWENTY-THIRD PSALM

The Lord is my shepherd,
I shall not want.

He makes me lie down
in green pastures.
He leads me beside still waters;
he restores my soul.

He guides me in
paths of righteousness
for his name's sake.

Even though I walk through
the valley of the shadow of death,
I fear no evil;
for you are with me;
your rod and
your staff comfort me.

You prepare a table before me
in the presence of my enemies.
You anoint my head with oil.
My cup overflows.

Surely goodness and love
shall follow me
all the days of my life.
And I shall live
in the house of the Lord
for ever.

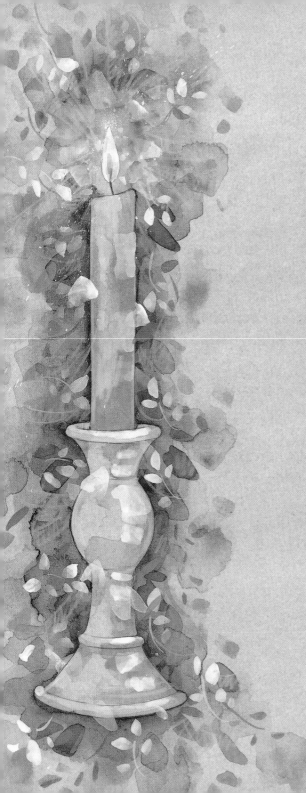

TRUST AND HOPE
IN THE EVENING

SAFE THROUGH THE NIGHT

Now I lay me down to sleep
I pray the Lord my soul to keep,
and keep me safe throughout the night,
and wake me with the morning light.

AT THE ENDING OF THIS DAY

O Lord my God,
I thank you at the ending of this day.
I thank you for rest of body and mind.
Your hand has been over me,
guarding and preserving me.
Forgive all my littleness of faith
and all the wrong I have done this day,
and help me to forgive all
who have done wrong to me.
Let me sleep in peace under your care.
I commit to you all whom I love,
all in this house,
and myself, both body and soul.
O God, praise be to your holy name.

Prayers of
Joy & Thanksgiving

THE DAY RETURNS

The day returns
and brings us the petty round
of irritating concerns and duties.
Help us to perform them
with laughter and kind faces.
Let cheerfulness
abound with industry.
Give us joy
in our business this day.
Bring us to our resting beds
weary and content
and undishonoured,
and grant us in the end
the gift of sleep.

PRAYER OF RICHARD OF CHICHESTER

Thanks be to you,
my Lord Jesus Christ,
for all the benefits which
you have given me;
for all the pains and insults
which you have borne for me,
O most merciful Redeemer,
Friend, and Brother.
May I know you more clearly,
love you more dearly,
and follow you more nearly.

34

God Makes the Difference

In all of our days
in so many wonderful,
beautiful ways,
the blessings he sends
from his own loving hand,
are better than anything
we could have planned.

His love for his children
is daily expressed;
like a father he gives
nothing less than his best.

His gifts and his goodness
fill life to the brim,
with a joy that could only
be fashioned by him.

A Grateful Heart

Lord, you have given
so much to me.
Give one thing more:
a grateful heart.

LOVE AND JOY

Live within my love.
When you obey me you are
living in my love,
just as I obey my Father
and live in his love.
I have told you this so that
you will be filled with joy.
Yes, your cup of joy will overflow!

JOHN 15:9-11

36

Prayers of
Sorrow & Anxiety

The Lord will turn
the darkness before you
into light.

ISAIAH 42:16

I am With You

Be strong and courageous.
Do not be afraid or discouraged,
for I, the Lord your God,
am with you wherever you go.

JOSHUA 1:9

When Dreams are Broken

When dreams are broken things
and joy has fled,
there is Jesus.
When hope is a struggle
and faith a fragile thread,
there is Jesus.

When grief is a shadow
and peace unknown,
there is Jesus.
When we need the assurance
that we're not alone,
there is Jesus.

Do Not Be Afraid

Do not be afraid, for I have redeemed you.
I have called you by your name; you are mine.

When you walk through the waters,
I'll be with you;
You will never sink beneath the waves.

When the fear of loneliness is looming,
then remember I am at your side.

You are mine, O my child, I am your Father,
and I love you with a perfect love.

BASED ON ISAIAH 43:1-5

Take Courage!

I can't change what you're going through,
I have no words to make a difference,
no answers or solutions
to make things easier for you.

But if it helps in any way
I want to say I care.

Please know that even when you're lonely
you're not alone.

I'll be here,
supporting you with all my thoughts,
cheering for you with all my strength,
praying for you with all my heart.

For whatever you need,
for as long as it takes –

Lean on my love.

You are No Stranger

You are no stranger
to my heavy heart, Lord.
You take upon yourself
the grief I bear.

I find strength and hope, Lord,
in your promise
that where I am,
you also will be there.

Beyond the Shadows

Let me look beyond the gathering shadows
of today, Lord.
Help me see tomorrow's hope,
even through my tears.
Shine your gentle sunlight on the winter
of my soul, Lord.
Warm my spirit with your love
until spring reappears.

You Are There

In this long night of my faith, Lord,
sorrow seems to have no end.
Yet I know the warmth and comfort
of a never failing friend.

So I rest, securely sheltered
in your love and gentle care,
knowing even in the darkness there is light.
For you are there.

God is the Answer

He comes as a Companion
to the lonely,
a Faithful Friend
who cares and understands.
He comes as a Physician
to the hurting,
with tenderness
and healing in his hands.

He comes as a Protector
to the helpless,
a Shepherd who calls
all his lambs by name,

a Father who sees
every child as special,
whose gentle heart
loves each of us the same.

He comes, the Consolation
of the suffering,
the Light that breaks
through darkness and despair.
He comes, and we discover
that his presence
is the loving answer to
our every prayer.

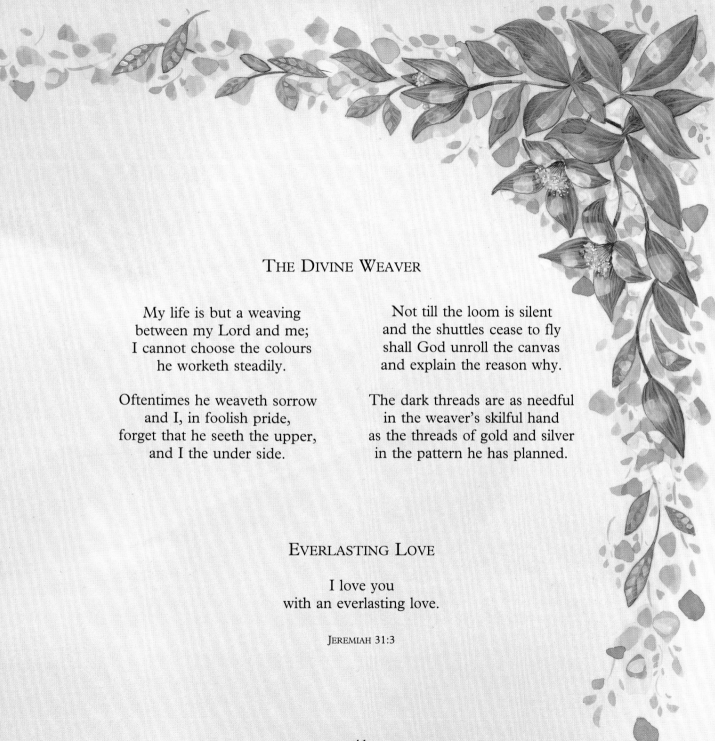

THE DIVINE WEAVER

My life is but a weaving
between my Lord and me;
I cannot choose the colours
he worketh steadily.

Oftentimes he weaveth sorrow
and I, in foolish pride,
forget that he seeth the upper,
and I the under side.

Not till the loom is silent
and the shuttles cease to fly
shall God unroll the canvas
and explain the reason why.

The dark threads are as needful
in the weaver's skilful hand
as the threads of gold and silver
in the pattern he has planned.

EVERLASTING LOVE

I love you
with an everlasting love.

JEREMIAH 31:3

FOOTPRINTS

One night I had a dream.
I dreamed I was walking along
the beach with God,
and across the sky flashed
scenes from my life. For each scene
I noticed two sets of footprints
in the sand, one belonged to me
and the other to God.

When the last scene of my life
flashed before me I looked back at
the footprints in the sand. I noticed
that at times along the path of life
there was only one set of footprints.

I also noticed that it happened at
the very lowest and saddest times
of my life. This really bothered me
and I questioned God about it.
'God, you said that once I decided
to follow you, you would walk
with me all the way, but I noticed
that during the most troublesome
times in my life there is only one
set of footprints. I don't understand
why in times when I needed you
most, you would leave me.'

God replied, 'My precious, precious child,
I love you and I would never, never
leave you during your times of
trials and suffering.
When you see only one set of footprints
it was then that I carried you.'

BEREAVEMENT

Do Not Be Sad

We want you to know the truth
about those who have died,
so that you will not be sad,
as are those who have no hope.
We believe that Jesus died and rose again;
so we believe that God will bring with Jesus
those who have died believing in him.

For this is the Lord's teaching, we tell you:
we who are alive on the day the Lord comes
will not go ahead of those who have died.

There will be a shout of command,
the archangel's voice,
the sound of God's trumpet,
and the Lord himself
will come down from heaven!
Those who have died believing in Christ
will be raised to life first;
then we who are living at that time
will be gathered up
along with them in the clouds
to meet the Lord in the air.
And so we will be always with the Lord.
Therefore cheer each other up with these words.

I Thessalonians 4:13-18

DEATH IS NOTHING AT ALL

Death is nothing at all.
I have only slipped away into the next room.
I am I, and you are you.
Whatever we were to each other,
that we still are.

Call me by my old familiar name,
speak to me in the easy way
which you always used.

Put no difference in your tone,
wear no forced air of solemnity or sorrow.
Laugh as we always laughed
at the little jokes we enjoyed together.

Let my name be ever the household word
that it always was,
let it be spoken without effect,
without the trace of a shadow on it.

Life means all that it ever meant.
It is the same as it ever was;
there is unbroken continuity.

Why should I be out of mind
because I am out of sight?

I am waiting for you,
for an interval,
somewhere very near,
just around the corner.

All is well.

HENRY SCOTT HOLLAND

BESIDE THE STILL WATERS

O God, my Father,
I know that you are afflicted
in all my afflictions;
and in my sorrow I come to you today
that you may give to me the comfort
which you alone can give.
Make me sure
that in perfect wisdom, perfect love,
and perfect power
you are working ever for the best.
Make me sure that a Father's hand
will never cause his child a needless tear.
Make me so sure of your love
that I will be able to
accept even that which I cannot understand.
Help me today to be thinking not of the
darkness of death,
but of the splendour of the life everlasting,
for ever in your presence
and for ever with you.

Help me still to face life with grace and gallantry
and help me to find courage to go on
in the memory that the best tribute
I can pay to my loved one
is not the tribute of tears,
but the constant memory
that another has been added
to the unseen cloud of witnesses
who compass us about.
Comfort and uphold me,
strengthen and support me,
until I also come to the green pastures
which are beside the still waters,
and until I meet again
those whom I have loved and lost awhile:
through Jesus Christ our Lord.

45

FROM THE LORD OF LOVE

My beloved,
these moments of sadness
are ones that I share with you.
My heart aches as yours.
How I long for you to know
the depth of my love for you at this time.
It is never easy to lose
that which is precious to you.
It is not easy to say goodbye
before one is ready.

Let me ease
these moments and comfort you.
I long to touch you
with the peace of my love.
Rest your weariness in me,
for I long to bear this burden for you.
Come, draw near to me.
Your heavenly Father.

In Comfort and in Hope

Weep, but briefly, for your loved ones
as they enter into the kingdom of God.
For they shall possess a joy and a peace
that is unavailable on God's earthly realm.
Rather, rejoice in their everlasting
and total happiness,
for their eyes have seen God.

Hold My Hand

Hold my hand, Lord.
Walk me through the loneliness
and the valley of my sorrow.
Hold onto me when I'm too afraid
to think about tomorrow.
Let me lean on you, Lord,
when I'm too weary to go on.
Hold my hand, Lord, through the night
until I see the light of dawn.

Those who live in the Lord never
see each other for the last time.

SYMPATHY

God be with you in your sorrow,
through the night and through the day;
may some blessing come tomorrow
that will clear its cloud away.

God is generous in his giving,
give him now the soul that's fled:
may he bless with strength the living,
rest eternally the dead.

LIFE ETERNAL

I am the Resurrection and the Life.
He who believes in me will live,
even though he dies;
and whoever lives and believes in me
will never die.

JOHN 11:25-26

Prayers for
Individuals & Families

MARRIAGE PRAYER

Lord, help us to remember
when we first met
and the strong love
that grew between us;
to work that love
into practical things
so nothing can divide us.
We ask for words
both kind and loving,
and hearts always ready
to ask for forgiveness
as well as to forgive.
Dear Lord,
we put our marriage
into your hands.

LEARNING TO LIVE

If a child lives with criticism
he learns to condemn.
If a child lives with hostility
he learns to fight.
If a child lives with ridicule
he learns to be shy.
If a child lives with shame
he learns to feel guilty.
If a child lives with tolerance
he learns to be patient.

If a child lives with encouragement
he learns confidence.
If a child lives with praise
he learns to appreciate.
If a child lives with fairness
he learns justice.
If a child lives with security
he learns to have faith.
If a child lives with approval
he learns to like himself.
If a child lives with acceptance
and friendship
he learns to find love in the world.

RECIPE FOR A HAPPY HOME

Combine happy hearts,
melt hearts into one,
add a lot of love.
Mix well with respect.
Add gentleness, laughter, joy,
faith, hope and self-control.
Pour in much understanding.
Don't forget the patience.
Blend in listening ears.
Allow to grow and share.
Sprinkle with smiles, hugs and kisses.
Bake for a lifetime.
Yield: One Happy Home!

BLESS OUR HOME

Bless our home, Father,
that we cherish the bread
before there is none,
discover each other
before we leave,
and enjoy each other
for what we are,
while we have time.

KITCHEN PRAYER

Lord of pots and pans and things,
since I've not the time to be a saint
by doing lovely things,
or watching late with thee,
or dreaming in the dawn light,
or storming heaven's gates,
make me a saint by getting meals
and washing up the plates.
Although I must have Martha's hands,
I have a Mary mind,
and when I black the boots and shoes
thy sandals, Lord, I find.
I think of how they trod the earth
what time I scrub the floor;
accept this meditation, Lord,
I haven't time for more.

GUIDE FOR A LOVING HOME

May we treat one another
with respect, honesty and care.
May we share the little discoveries
and changes each day brings.
May we try always to be sensitive
to one another's joys, sorrows,
needs and changing moods,
and realise that being
a loving family means
sometimes not understanding
everyone all the time
but being there to love
and help them just the same.

IF I COULD

If I could, I would teach each child to be positive,
    to smile, to love and be loved.

I would teach each child to take time
to observe some miracle of nature –
    the song of a bird,
    the beauty of a snowflake,
the orange glow of a winter sunset.

I would teach each child to feel warmly
about those for whom the task of learning
    does not come easily.

I would teach each one to be kind
    to all living creatures
and to crowd out of their lives
feelings of guilt, misunderstanding
    and lack of compassion.

I would teach each child that it is alright
to show their feelings by laughing,
crying, or touching someone they care about.

Everyday I would have a child feel special
    and through my actions,
each one would know how much
    I really care.

A Prayer for Those Who Live Alone

I live alone, dear Lord,
stay by my side;
in all my daily needs
be thou my guide.
Grant me good health,
for that indeed I pray,
to carry on my work
from day to day.

Keep pure my mind,
my thoughts, my every deed,
let me be kind, unselfish,
in my neighbour's need.
Spare me from fire, from flood,
malicious tongues,
from thieves, from fear,
and evil ones.

If sickness or an accident befall,
then humbly, Lord, I pray,
hear thou my call.
And when I'm feeling low,
or in despair,
lift up my heart
and help me in my prayer.

I live alone, dear Lord,
yet have no fear,
because I feel your presence
ever near.

Together we can
do something beautiful
for God.

Mother Teresa

Blessings

When You're Lonely

When you're lonely,
I wish you love.

When you're down,
I wish you joy.

When you're troubled,
I wish you peace.

When things are complicated,
I wish you simple beauty.

When things look empty,
I wish you hope.

A Blessing

May the Lord bless you
and take care of you;

May the Lord be kind
and gracious to you;

May the Lord look on you with favour
and give you peace.

NUMBERS 6:22-27

THE PEACE OF GOD

Have no anxiety about anything
but in everything,
by prayer and supplication,
with thanksgiving, let your requests
be made known to God.

And the peace of God,
which passes all understanding,
will keep your hearts and your minds
in Christ Jesus.

PHILIPPIANS 4:4-7

PAUL'S FAREWELL

Be happy
and grow in Christ.

Do what I have said,
and live in harmony
and peace.

May the grace of our Lord
Jesus Christ
be with you all.

May God's love,
and the Holy Spirit's
friendship,
be yours.

2 CORINTHIANS 13:11-14

LOVING CARE

May God,
who understands each need,
who listens to every prayer,
bless you and keep you
in his loving, tender care.

I SAID A PRAYER

I said a prayer for you today
and know God must have heard –
I felt the answer in my heart
although he spoke no word!
I didn't ask for wealth or fame
(I knew you wouldn't mind) –
I asked him to send treasures
of a far more lasting kind!

I asked that he'd be near you
at the start of each new day
to grant you health and blessings
and friends to share your way!
I asked for happiness for you
in all things great and small –
but it was for his loving care
I prayed the most of all!

THE BEATITUDES

Blessed are the poor in spirit,
for theirs is the kingdom of heaven.

Blessed are those who mourn,
for they shall be comforted.

Blessed are the meek,
for they shall inherit the earth.

Blessed are those who hunger
and thirst for righteousness,
for they shall be satisfied.

Blessed are the merciful,
for they shall obtain mercy.

Blessed are the pure in heart,
for they shall see God.

Blessed are the peacemakers,
for they shall be called
sons of God.

Blessed are those who are persecuted
for righteousness' sake,
for theirs is the kingdom of heaven.

MATTHEW 5:3-10

Deep Peace

Deep peace of the Running Wave to you.
Deep peace of the Flowing Air to you.
Deep peace of the Quiet Earth to you.
Deep peace of the Shining Stars to you.
Deep peace of the Son of Peace to you.

Celtic Benediction

His Love

May his love enfold you.
May his peace surround you.
May his light touch you.

60

A Subject Index

ACCEPTANCE
God grant me serenity 18
Help me to accept 23
Life's lessons 26
Beside the still waters 45
Learning to live 50
Kitchen prayer 51
Be at peace 20

ANSWERS TO PRAYER
The Difference 8
I asked Jesus 12
God is the answer 40
Take courage! 39
I said a prayer 58

ANXIETY
Remind me, Lord 21
The fruit of the Spirit 12
From a friend 10
The peace of God 57
Where God is 22
Be at peace 20

ASSURANCE
Christ is the bridge 17
Safe in God's keeping 23
The Gate of the Year 28
You are there 40
When dreams are broken 38
Where God is 22
Be at peace 20

BEAUTY
God makes the difference 35
If I could 53
Together we can do 54
When you're lonely 56

BLESSING
Friendship 13
God makes the difference 35
Sympathy 48
Bless our home 51
Be at peace 20

CARE
God for us
From a friend 10
A messenger of your love 15
Lord, your way is perfect 24
At the ending of this day 32
The fruit of the Spirit 12
You are there 40
God is the answer 40
Take courage! 39
I said a prayer 58
A blessing 56
Loving care 58
Be at peace 20

Us for each other
Simple acts of love 13
Never too busy to care 14
A messenger of your love 15

Someone who cares 14
Take courage! 39
If I could 53
Guide for a loving home 52

COMMITMENT
From a friend 10
A Prayer of dedication 15
Prayer of Francis of Assisi 16
Trust in God 25
Life's lessons 26
At the ending of this day 32
Your will be done 29

CONTENTMENT
Lord, your way is perfect 24
The day returns 34
Where God is 22
Be at peace 20

COURAGE
God grant me serenity 18
I am with you always 29
Do not be afraid 38
Take courage! 39
Beside the still waters 45
Be at peace 20

CREATION
Christ is the bridge 17
If I could 53
Deep peace 60
From a friend 10
The Twenty-Third Psalm 31

DEATH
Friendship 13
The Twenty-Third Psalm 31
Sympathy 48
Life eternal 48
Death is nothing at all 44
Do not be sad 43
Beside the still waters 45

DOUBT AND DESPAIR
A prayer for patience 18
Don't quit 25
Footprints 42
God is the answer 40
You are there 40
A prayer for those who
live alone 54

ENCOURAGEMENT
The day returns 34
Take courage! 39
Learning to live 50
Be at peace 20

ETERNITY
Friendship 13
Sympathy 48
Life eternal 48
Do not be sad 43

Beside the still waters 45
In comfort and in hope 47

EVENING
May your love 21
The Lord our protector 21
The Gate of the Year 28
Wings of Faith 30
At the ending of this day 32
Safe through the night 32
The fruit of the Spirit 12
From a friend 10
Sympathy 48
His love 60
Be at peace 20
Safe in God's keeping 23
Be Still 20

FAITH
The fruit of the Spirit 12
From a friend 10
Prayer of dedication 15
Prayer of Francis of Assisi 16
Where God is 22
I am with you always 29
Trust in God 25
Life's lessons 26
Wings of Faith 30
At the ending of this day 32
Do not be afraid 38
You are there 40
When dreams are broken 38
Life eternal 48
Do not be sad 43
Learning to live 50
Recipe for a happy home 51
Be at peace 20

FAMILY
At the ending of this day 32
If I could 53
Learning to live 50

FORGIVENESS
The Lord's Prayer 6
Love 12
At the ending of this day 32
Marriage prayer 50

FRIENDSHIP
Take time 7
From a friend 10
Friendship 13
Someone who cares 14
Christ be with me 28
Prayer of Richard of Chichester 34
God is the answer 40
You are there 40
Learning to live 50
I said a prayer 58
Paul's Farewell 57

GENTLENESS
The fruit of the Spirit 12
Recipe for a happy home 51

GIFTS (OF GOD)

The Lord's Prayer — 6
Take time — 7
From a friend — 10
Give me patience — 18
Your will for my life — 22
Jesus is pleased to come — 26
Life's lessons — 26
Wings of Faith — 30
A grateful heart — 35
The day returns — 34
Prayer of Richard of Chichester — 34
God makes the difference — 35
The fruit of the Spirit — 12
From a friend — 10
Footprints — 42
Sympathy — 48
Beside the still waters — 45
A blessing — 56
Where God is — 22

GIVING (BY US)

Prayer of dedication — 15
Prayer of Francis of Assisi — 16
Jesus is pleased to come — 26
Your will be done — 29

GRACE

God has not promised — 20
Life's lessons — 26
A prayer when distracted — 27
A blessing — 56
Paul's Farewell — 57

GROWING

Prayer of dedication — 15
Give me patience — 18
Help me to accept — 23
Life's lessons — 26
Recipe for a happy home — 51
Paul's farewell — 57

GUIDANCE

The Lord's Prayer — 6
Peace — 16
The Twenty-Third Psalm — 31

HAPPINESS

Take time — 7
In comfort and in hope — 47
Recipe for a happy home — 51
I said a prayer — 58
Paul's Farewell — 57

HELP AND HEALING

The Difference — 8
Friendship — 13
Someone who cares — 14
A prayer for patience — 18
The Lord our protector — 21
God has not promised — 20
Lord, your way is perfect — 24
Together — 24
Life's lessons — 26

The day returns — 34
God is the answer — 40
Take courage! — 39
Beyond the shadows — 39
Beside the still waters — 45
A prayer for those who
    live alone — 54
Guide for a loving home — 52
Marriage prayer — 50
I said a prayer — 58
Where God is — 22
Be at peace — 20

HOPE

When dreams are broken — 38
You are no stranger — 39
Beyond the shadows — 39
Do not be sad — 43
In comfort and in hope — 47
When you're lonely — 56

HUMILITY

The fruit of the Spirit — 12
Make me willing — 14
A prayer for those who
    live alone — 54
The Beatitudes — 59

JOURNEY OF LIFE

A prayer of dedication — 15
Christ is the bridge — 17
God has not promised — 20
Lord, your way is perfect — 24
I am with you always — 29
The Twenty-Third Psalm — 31
The Gate of the Year — 28
Don't quit — 25
Prayer of Richard of Chichester — 34
Do not be afraid — 38
Footprints — 42
Hold my hand — 47
I said a prayer — 58

JOY AND LAUGHTER

Take time — 7
A Prayer for patience — 18
God has not promised — 20
The day returns — 34
Love and joy — 36
God makes the difference — 35
Recipe for a happy home — 51

KINDNESS

The day returns — 34
A Prayer for those who
    live alone — 54
If I could — 53
Marriage prayer — 50

KINGDOM OF GOD

The Lord's Prayer — 6
In comfort and in hope — 47
The Beatitudes — 59
Where God is — 22

LEARNING AND TEACHING

A prayer for patience — 18
Life's lessons — 26
Don't quit — 25
Your will be done — 29
Do not be sad — 43
If I could — 53
Learning to live — 50

LIFE

Prayer of Francis of Assisi — 16
Peace — 16
The Lord our protector — 21
Your will for my life — 22
Help me to accept — 23
Jesus is pleased to come — 26
I am with you always — 29
The Twenty-Third Psalm — 31
Life's lessons — 26
Don't quit — 25
An everyday prayer — 26
A prayer when distracted — 27
God makes the difference — 35
Footprints — 42
The Divine Weaver — 41
Life eternal — 48
Recipe for a happy home — 51

LISTENING

From a friend — 10
Prayer for patience — 18
Recipe for a happy home — 51

LIVING

Prayer of dedication — 15
Peace — 16
Jesus is pleased to come — 26
The Twenty-Third Psalm — 31
Love and joy — 36
Life eternal — 48
Those who live in the Lord — 48
A prayer for those who
    live alone — 54
If I could — 53
Learning to live — 50
Paul's Farewell — 57
Be at peace — 20

LONELINESS

Never too busy to care — 14
Do not be afraid — 38
God is the answer — 40
Take courage! — 39
Hold my hand — 47
When you're lonely — 56

LOVE

God for us

Christ is the bridge — 17
Safe in God's keeping — 23
May your love — 21
Remind me, Lord — 21
Jesus is pleased to come — 26
Prayer of Richard of Chichester — 34

Love and joy 36
God makes the difference 35
Do not be afraid 38
Footprints 42
Everlasting love 41
God is the answer 40
You are there 40
Take courage! 39
Beyond the shadows 39
From the Lord of love 46
I said a prayer 58
Paul's Farewell 57
His love 60

Us for each other

Take time 7
Prayer of Francis of Assisi 16
Jesus is pleased to come 26
Life's lessons 26
Take courage! 39
In comfort and in hope 47
If I could 53
Learning to live 50
Guide for a loving home 52
Marriage prayer 50
Recipe for a happy home 51

MERCY
Trust the past 19
The Twenty-Third Psalm 31
A prayer when distracted 27
Prayer of Richard of Chichester 34
The Beatitudes 59

MORNING
The Difference 8
Your will for my life 22
Together 24
An everyday prayer 26
The Lord's Prayer 6
The day returns 34
I said a prayer 58
Take time 7
From a friend 10
Never too busy to care 14
Prayer of dedication 15
A messenger of your love 15
Someone who cares 14
Trust in God 25

NEED
The Lord's Prayer 6
Never too busy to care 14
The Twenty-Third Psalm 31
God makes the difference 35
Footprints 42
When dreams are broken 38
Take courage! 39
A prayer for those who
live alone 54
Guide for a loving home 52
Bless our home 51

OPENNESS AND OBEDIENCE
A prayer when distracted 27
Love and joy 36

PATIENCE
Love 12
A prayer for patience 18
Give me patience 18
Learning to live 50
Recipe for a happy home 51

PEACE
A messenger of your love 15
Be at peace 20
Prayer of Francis of Assisi 16
Peace 16
Christ is the bridge 17
Where God is 22
May your love 21
God has not promised 20
Jesus is pleased to come 26
I am with you 38
A prayer when distracted 27
The fruit of the Spirit 12
From a friend 10
When dreams are broken 38
From the Lord of love 46
In comfort and in hope 47
The Beatitudes 59
Deep peace 60
A blessing 56
The peace of God 57
When you're lonely 56
Paul's Farewell 57
His love 60

PLANNING
Thy will 24
An everyday prayer 26
God makes the difference 35
The Divine Weaver 41
Be at peace 20

PRAYER
The Lord's Prayer 6
Take time 7
The Difference 8
From a friend 10
A prayer of dedication 15
God is the answer 40
Kitchen prayer 51
I said a prayer 58
The peace of God 57

PRESENCE OF GOD
The Difference 8
From a friend 10
I am with you 38
The Twenty-Third Psalm 31
Prayer of Richard of Chichester 34
God is the answer 40
From the Lord of love 46
Beside the still waters 45

A prayer for those who
live alone 54
Be at peace 20
I said a prayer 58
The peace of God 57
Where God is 22

PROMISE
God has not promised 20
You are no stranger 39
Be at peace 20

PROVIDENCE
The Lord our protector 21
God is the answer 40
You are there 40
Trust the past 19
I am with you always 29
Life's lessons 26
The day returns 34
The fruit of the Spirit 12
From a friend 10
Do not be sad 43
Be at peace 20

PURITY
A prayer for those who
live alone 54
The Beatitudes 59

QUIET
Lord, your way is perfect 24
Christ be with me 28
A Prayer when distracted 27
Deep peace 60
Be still 20
The Twenty-Third Psalm 31
Where God is 22
Be at peace 20

REDEMPTION
Prayer of Richard of Chichester 34
Do not be afraid 38
I asked Jesus 12
Love 12
Prayer of Francis of Assisi 16
Peace 16
The Lord our protector 21
The Twenty-Third Psalm 31
Do not be sad 43
Hold my hand 47

REST
God has not promised 20
The Twenty-Third Psalm 31
An everyday prayer 26
A prayer when distracted 27
At the ending of this day 32
The day returns 34
You are there 40
From the Lord of love 46

RIGHTEOUSNESS
The Twenty-Third Psalm 31
The Beatitudes 59

SENSITIVITY
Never too busy to care 14
Guide for a loving home 52

SERVICE
Make me willing 14
Your will be done 29
Take time 7
Simple acts of love 13
Never too busy to care 14
Prayer of dedication 15
A messenger of your love 15
The day returns 34
Together we can do 54
Kitchen prayer 51

SHARING
Guide for a loving home 52
Recipe for a happy home 51
I said a prayer 58

SIMPLICITY
Simple acts of love 13
Never too busy to care 14
Lord, your way is perfect 24
When you're lonely 56

SOLITUDE
Give me patience 18
A prayer for those who
live alone 54

SORROW AND SUFFERING
God has not promised 20
The Twenty-Third Psalm 31
Christ be with me 28
Wings of Faith 30
A prayer when distracted 27
The Beatitudes 59

STRENGTH
God has not promised 20
Life's lessons 26
I am with you 38
The fruit of the Spirit 12
From a friend 10
You are no stranger 39
Take courage! 39
Sympathy 48
Beside the still waters 45

SUCCESS
Take time 7
Trust in God 25
Don't quit 25

SYMPATHY
God has not promised 20
Sympathy 48

THANKSGIVING
At the ending of this day 32
Prayer of Richard of Chichester 34
The peace of God 57

TIME
Take time 7
The Difference 8
A prayer for patience 18
If I could 53
Kitchen prayer 51
Recipe for a happy home 51

TRIALS AND TROUBLES
The Difference 8
Remind me, Lord 21
God has not promised 20
Footprints 42
When you're lonely 56
Don't quit 25
When dreams are broken 38

TRUST
From a friend 10
Prayer of dedication 15
Prayer of Francis of Assisi 16
Peace 16
Be at peace 20

TRUTH
Love 12
Peace 16
Jesus is pleased to come 26

WAR
Peace 16
Christ is the bridge 17

WISDOM
Take time 7
God grant me serenity 18
Beside the still waters 45

WORK
Take time 7
The Difference 8
Never too busy to care 14
God has not promised 20
Trust in God 25
A prayer when distracted 27
Your will be done 29
The day returns 34
A prayer for those who
live alone 54